Everything You Need to Know About

Being a Baby-Sitter

A Teen's Guide to Responsible Child Care

Baby-sitting can be fun and rewarding for both the baby-sitter and the children he or she is looking after.

Everything You Need to Know About

Being a Baby-Sitter

A Teen's Guide to Responsible Child Care

Aileen Weintraub

The Rosen Publishing Group, Inc.
New York

To my parents, Lois and Richard, for their encouragement, and to the Kamaras family for their inspiration

Published in 2000, 2003 by The Rosen Publishing Group, Inc.
29 East 21st Street, New York, NY 10010

Copyright © 2000, 2003 by The Rosen Publishing Group, Inc.

Revised Edition 2003

Library of Congress Cataloging-in-Publication Data
Weintraub, Aileen, 1973–
Everything you need to know about being a baby-sitter / Aileen Weintraub.
   p.   cm.—(The need to know library)
Includes bibliographical references and index.
Summary: Discusses the responsibilities and challenges of being a baby-sitter, including child care, staying safe, handling emergencies, negotiating, and networking.
ISBN 0-8239-3770-4 (lib. bdg.)
1. Babysitting Handbooks, manuals, etc. Juvenile literature.
2. Babysitting Handbooks, manuals, etc. Juvenile literature.
[1. Babysitters Handbooks, manuals, etc.]
I. Title. II. Series.
HQ769.5.W45 1999
649'.1'0248—dc21
99-36045 CIP
Manufactured in the United States of America

Contents

As a baby-sitter, you can earn extra money while enjoying fun times playing with children.

Introduction

Baby-sitting is a great way for teens to earn extra money after school and on weekends. It can be very rewarding—not to mention a lot of fun for both you and the children you look after. As a baby-sitter, you get to play outside in the fresh air with the children, read them bedtime stories, and dream up games, activities, and arts-and-crafts projects.

Baby-sitting isn't just fun and games, however. Taking care of someone else's pride and joy requires a lot of responsibility and hard work. There are many factors to keep in mind before you accept a baby-sitting job. You have to be friendly and fun to keep the kids happy, but you also have to be mature and in control so that the parents trust you and feel confident calling you for more business. Being a good baby-sitter demands a great deal of patience, as you will have to deal with the ever changing and often unpredictable needs of children.

Like any other job, baby-sitting requires a certain amount of training. As you will see in chapter 1, there are many aspects of baby-sitting to be learned. It is also important to learn how to handle emergencies and to know whom to contact in potentially risky situations. Chapter 2 offers safety tips as well as advice on what to do in child care emergencies.

Coming up with fun activities for the kids is often the baby-sitter's favorite part of the job, but even the most experienced sitters sometimes run out of ideas. Chapter 3 offers suggestions for keeping children of all ages entertained.

Chapter 4 covers one of the toughest aspects of baby-sitting: enforcing discipline. What do you do when the children won't listen to you, or when they fight with one another? How can you earn a child's respect while also being a friend?

With all of these responsibilities to think about, it is easy to forget that as a baby-sitter, you have certain rights. Chapter 5 discusses what these rights are and how to ensure that they are respected by your employers. Learning how to negotiate or decide on a fee for your services is a crucial first step. In addition, you need to make sure that you feel comfortable in the family's house and that you have a safe way to get home if you are planning to leave after dark.

Baby-sitting opens up a whole new world of opportunities. You might even begin to consider pursuing a career in child care. This field includes a wide variety of jobs, some of which are discussed in chapter 6. In addition, baby-sitting is good practice if you decide to have children of your own someday.

Good baby-sitters are hard to find. Once you prove yourself to be responsible, friendly, and fun, your employer will probably want to keep you and will try to make the job worth your while. This book shows you how to be a super sitter and how to let others know just how good you are. With hard work, patience, and a little innovation, you will be on your way to a successful baby-sitting business in no time!

Baby-sitters must be honest and responsible.
Trustworthy baby-sitters are always in high demand.

Chapter 1

The Basics of Baby-Sitting

As you begin to take on assignments and gain experience as a baby-sitter, you will learn that the job involves a lot more than simply watching a child for a few hours to make extra pocket money.

Baby-sitting is a major responsibility, one of the biggest responsibilities you will have in life. Unlike most jobs, where you are accountable for tracking inventory, stocking shelves, or keeping records, baby-sitting puts you in the position of being responsible for the health, safety, and happiness of a living, breathing person. There is nothing like having a child depend on you for safety and comfort. The experience will give you more self-confidence, which will follow you throughout your life, helping you excel in school, career, and family. But before you begin, there are some basics of the job you should be familiar with.

Characteristics of a Good Baby-Sitter

Generally, as a baby-sitter you should be able to work well under pressure. You will encounter many stressful situations on the job. The test is how well you manage them. When the child you are baby-sitting cries, will you be able to calm him or her down? When the child wants to watch television late into the night or refuses to eat, will you be able to handle the situation? You may have to change diapers, prepare special food, and attend to illness if you are taking care of a younger child. Will this be a problem for you? In an emergency, will you be able to think clearly and take command of the situation? Patience, understanding, and keeping calm are the basic characteristics of a good baby-sitter. But there are others you should focus on as well.

Good Health

Most important, you should be healthy as a baby-sitter. By staying healthy, you are also ensuring the health of the child, since children, especially those under the age of three, are vulnerable to infection and illness. It also takes longer for them to recover if they do get sick. What may be only a common cold to you can turn out to be a serious illness to a child. If you are coughing, sneezing, feeling feverish, or queasy, call in sick. The parents will understand and will be glad that you warned them.

Responsibility and Dependability

Being responsible means that you will make the right decisions to avoid emergency situations. Being dependable means that should an emergency situation arise, you will make the right choices to best handle the problem. Being dependable is especially important because there are some emergencies that simply cannot be avoided. If you are responsible and dependable, the parents will know their child will be safe in any situation.

Love for Children

Children generally have a good sense of how people feel about them. If you enjoy being around, playing games with, and talking to children, they will know and feel the same way toward you. On the other hand, if you are watching them only for the money or as a favor and show that you would rather be out with friends or at home, children will pick up on this as well. In order to have a fun and fulfilling time as a baby-sitter, a love for children is necessary.

Knowledge of Children

Children are not all alike, especially those of different ages. Since you will probably be taking care of a variety of children, you should understand the different stages of their development. You should also know the basic techniques of feeding, dressing, diapering, bathing, and playing with both younger and older children.

make the right choices. As a baby-sitter, you will sooner or later face a situation where you are unsure whether your decision is the right one. Being self-confident will allow you to be more sure that you are handling these situations in the right way.

Good Manners

Good manners can take you a long way in any profession. Though it may not seem so, people remember when you say thank-you, smile, or hold a door open for them. Not only do they remember the gestures, they remember you. When looking for a baby-sitter next time or recommending one to a friend, parents will remember you because of your politeness. A simple handshake can lead the way to more jobs down the road and a successful baby-sitting business.

As you can tell, there is a lot more to baby-sitting than simply watching children. To be a good baby-sitter takes a great amount of skill. Even if you feel that you have a lot to learn, don't get discouraged. To become good at anything takes practice. The more children you baby-sit, the more you will learn what it takes to make them feel most comfortable when their parents are away. The lessons you learn will make the job well worth the effort.

Chapter 2

Safety First

Noah is baby-sitting for Edward and Andrea. Andrea, who is seven years old, starts chasing Edward, who is only four. At first both are enjoying themselves, playing hide-and-seek, crawling under tables, and running from room to room in the house. Noah tells them not to run inside the house, and, for a few minutes, the children settle down.

But soon Andrea is tackling her brother, and Edward, trying to escape, jumps up on the couch. Edward continues jumping up and down on the sofa cushions while Noah explains to Andrea that she needs to calm down and play nicely. Suddenly there is a loud thud, and

Edward begins to scream. Noah quickly turns around to find that Edward has fallen off the couch and has hit his head on the coffee table. Noah rushes over to the wailing child to inspect the damage. He scoops up Edward off the floor and sees a big red welt forming on the child's head. Noah realizes that this is a potentially dangerous situation. Staying calm, he quickly takes the child to the kitchen, where he finds an ice pack. Noah holds the ice to Edward's head and tells Andrea to choose a book from the shelf to read quietly until Edward stops crying.

Taking Precautions

Most children are resilient and bounce back easily from accidents. As a baby-sitter, you will probably deal mostly with minor cuts and bruises. Children frequently bump into things, scrape their knees and elbows, and fall down. Chances are, even if there is some blood and a lot of screaming, you are not looking at a major tragedy. However, there are occasions when a Band-Aid and some sympathy just aren't enough. It is important to be prepared for these emergency situations.

The simplest precautions can help save a child's life. The first thing to do before the parents leave the house is to make sure that they have provided a list of important telephone numbers. This list should include

It is vital for baby-sitters to know how to handle accidents and to know whom to call for help in an emergency.

numbers for the police and fire departments, the family physician, poison control, and at least two trustworthy neighbors. In addition, parents should always leave a number where they can be reached in case of an emergency. This list can come in handy. You don't want to have to worry about looking up numbers in the phone book when a child's life is in danger.

It is also a good idea to ask the parents where they keep first-aid items such as Band-Aids, antiseptics, creams, and ice packs. If they don't have many supplies, tell them that you would feel more comfortable watching their children if the medicine cabinet were kept fully stocked. Find out if the children you are caring for have any allergies to certain foods or medications and inquire about any special diets or medicine regimens. In addition, it is important to be aware of any medical conditions a child might have, such as asthma or diabetes.

Different Types of Emergencies

It is not always necessary to call parents about minor injuries such as cuts and scrapes. However, it is important to let them know when they return home what happened in their absence. If they find a mysterious bruise or cut on their child, they are going to wonder what happened and where it came from. Here are some safety tips to read over before you begin baby-sitting:

◎ **If a child suddenly develops a fever or starts vomiting, first call the parents and then the doctor. The parents will decide whether they feel the need to return home. Remember, the child is theirs. It is best to let them make the decision.**

◎ **If a child ingests a poisonous substance such as bleach or paint, don't waste any time. Call poison control immediately. This department is specially trained to handle these types of situations and will** know better than a hospital or the child's parents what to do.

◎ If there is a possibility that a child has broken a bone or needs stitches, try to keep him or her as still as possible. Call an adult, such as a neighbor, for assistance. Be very gentle when handling the child. If you think that the child may have a broken bone, try not to touch him or her at all. Attempting to move a child who has a broken bone will not only hurt him or her but can potentially make the injury worse. If the child is bleeding, apply pressure to the wound with a cloth. If you think that the child needs to go to the hospital, get him or her there as quickly as possible and call the parents at the first opportunity. Chances are that a hospital will not operate on a child without a parent's consent.

◎ It is a very good idea to take a CPR or emergency first-aid class at your school or local community center. This is good training to have not only because it can help save lives, but also because it shows potential employers that you are concerned with the well-being of their children.

◎ Fire safety is another issue that people often fail to think about until it is too late. Be aware of all exits in a house and ask the parents if all of the fire alarms and smoke detectors are in good condition. Also suggest that they keep a fire extinguisher by the stove, and make sure never to let a child near a hot appliance. If a fire should occur, the first thing to do is to get the children out of the house. Call the fire department from a neighbor's house. Remember, the children are your number-one concern.

Other Safety Tips

Bath time can be lots of fun, but it can involve extra work for you—as well as extra risks for the child. If the parents want their child to have a bath while you are baby-sitting, make sure that you feel comfortable with the responsibility involved. Many accidents occur in the bathtub. It can take only a few seconds for a child to drown, even in very shallow water.

Make sure that the water is warm but not too hot. Don't fill up the tub all the way; halfway or less should do depending on the age and size of the child. Never leave the child unattended, even for a second. If the child is older and demands privacy, stay outside and talk to the child every few minutes to see how he or she is doing.

You must also remember never to leave an infant unattended on a changing table. If you need to leave the table for any reason, take the child with you. Even a small infant can roll off the table. Infants are extremely fragile and have very soft skulls, so take extra care when handling them. When placing an infant in a crib, it is preferable to lay the child on his or her back, making sure that there are no toys or heavy blankets that can suffocate the child. Always support an infant's head and neck when picking him or her up.

You may want to ask the parents to put a monitor in the baby's room so that you can hear his or her movements when you are in other parts of the house. Also be aware that very young children love to put things in their mouths. It takes only a few seconds for a child to choke, so keep an eye on young children at all times. During mealtimes, it is a good idea to cut food into small pieces for younger children so that they can chew more easily.

When playing with children, both indoors and outdoors, never let them wander too far away from you. If you are in the park and a stranger approaches a child under your care, immediately go over to the child. You may want to ask the parents if the child knows never to talk to strangers. If a stranger comes to the door while you are baby-sitting, under no circumstance should you let him or her in the house. If the person says that he or she is a family friend, politely explain that you were not told to expect anyone and that it would be best if he or she could come back later. Tell the person that you are willing to take a message and that you will be sure to tell the parents of his or her visit. This is also how you should handle visits from plumbers, electricians, and any other people whom you don't know personally.

When a Child Doesn't Return Home

If you are expecting a child to return home from school or from a play date with a friend and he or she doesn't show up on time, call the school or the friend's home to see if the child has left yet. If the child doesn't come home and nobody has seen him or her for a while, call the parents to let them know the situation and then call the local police.

It is a good idea to look around the neighborhood yourself after you have made these important calls. The child may have stopped at the candy store or the video arcade. If you decide to do this, make sure that a trustworthy neighbor comes over and waits by the phone in case the child calls or shows up at the house. Explain to the children, and regularly remind them, that they should call you if they are ever going to be late for any reason, even if it is a matter of only a few minutes. Also let them know that they should come directly home without stopping anywhere.

Baby-sitting emergencies are not everyday occurrences, but when they do happen, it is vital that you act quickly and calmly. Do not panic. This will only make things worse. If you stay in control of the situation, not only will the children feel more secure, but you will get through the crisis much more easily. Keep in mind that an occasional accident does not mean that you are a bad baby-sitter. And whatever the situation—whether it's sibling rivalry, a playground accident, or a suspicious stranger—always keep the parents well informed.

Chapter 3

Fun and Games

Yurgos is pacing back and forth in the living room, bored because he has nothing to do. He misses his mother and feels restless. He turns on the television, but nothing good is on. Then he looks through his bookshelf, but he has already read all of the books there.

He wanders into the kitchen where Charles, his baby-sitter, is finishing up washing the lunch dishes. Yurgos pulls out a chair from the kitchen table and sits down. Charles knows that Yurgos is restless but doesn't really know what to do about it. Yurgos is nine years old and doesn't like some of the activities that younger children enjoy.

Charles sits down at the kitchen table with Yurgos and tries to start a conversation. Yurgos is not interested in talking to Charles. When Charles asks him what he would like to do, Yurgos does not have any ideas. Charles realizes that he has to think of a good idea on his own. It will be at least another three hours before Yurgos's parents come home, and Charles does not want to sit around with a miserable child for all that time.

He begins suggesting a few things to Yurgos, including playing video games, going for a walk, and starting a project. But Yurgos just sits there, looking as miserable as ever. Finally, Charles gets up and goes to the hall closet. He comes back with a bat and ball and announces that they are going to the park. Suddenly Yurgos livens up. Charles realizes that all he has to do is show some excitement and be persistent, and he will eventually find something that they are both interested in doing.

Baby-sitting is a job to be taken seriously, but this does not mean that it is all work and no play. Interacting with the children is an important part of developing a good relationship with the whole family. If the children think of you as a fun person, not only are they more likely to respect and listen to you, they may end up requesting you as their baby-sitter of choice.

Baby-sitting is not just about making sure that the kids are safe, although that is a big part of it. It is about making sure that they are happy as well. You may find

Keeping a child entertained and happy is a challenging experience, but it can be very rewarding.

that you enjoy spending quality time with the kids you are baby-sitting and that it helps you understand their behavior and their personalities. Playing with the children on their level also helps them gain trust in you.

No matter what age the children are, there are many fun things to do with them. Most kids have plenty of toys of their own and will usually know exactly which ones they are in the mood to play with. Sometimes all you have to do is sit on the floor with the kids and follow their directions. At other times, children become bored with the toys they have. Children are usually very imaginative, but sometimes they need some help making up new games. That's where you come in.

Imaginative Ideas

A great way to get—and keep—a child's attention is to bring a "creativity box" with you. Children love new things and will be intrigued by the goodies you bring. Fill a shoe box with arts-and-crafts supplies, including construction paper, magic markers, glue, safety scissors, buttons, beads, pipe cleaners, empty paper-towel rolls, old socks (clean, of course!), and yarn. With these materials you can make silly puppets, funny animals, wild necklaces, or works of art to hang up on the refrigerator.

If you are baby-sitting around mealtime, letting the children help you cook can be fun. Depending on their dexterity and under your close supervision, they can

Since everything is new and exciting to them, babies can be entertained with safe toys like mobiles.

help set the table, stir the vegetables, or pour the juice. Baking is also a fun and easy activity. Check with the parents first; if they approve, ask them to keep brownie or chocolate chip cookie mix in the house. Kids will be happy stirring the ingredients together and licking the bowl. Making ice cream sundaes is another fun activity that most kids can't refuse. Be careful not to overdo the sweets, however. Ask the parents about any meal or dessert rules they might have.

Some older children prefer to stay by themselves. Don't take this personally. Everyone needs to be alone sometimes. Infants and toddlers, on the other hand, may require more playtime with you. Since everything is new and exciting to them, they can be distracted for reasonable periods of time with mobiles, small stuffed animals, music boxes, or anything with bright colors. Remember, though, that if given the opportunity, babies will put everything into their mouths, so give them only soft plush items that are not small enough to be swallowed. Some babies are content just to be held but have a limited attention span and may get fussy. Talk to the infant and make funny faces. You don't have to be a rock star for them to appreciate your singing, as long as it is not too loud. Babies don't like startling sounds, as they are still getting used to their environment.

Toddlers love to run around and are always getting into things, so it is especially important to keep a close eye on them. You can turn on the stereo and encourage them to dance around to music. Many toddlers also love playing with dolls or building blocks and using coloring books. Often they know exactly what they want to play with, but they might still need your assistance. Let the child guide you to the games he or she wants to play, and always act enthusiasticly.

Other indoor activities that keep children happy include watching videos and reading books. Encouraging older children to read to you can be both fun and educational. These are good nighttime activities that can help children wind down before going to bed.

Outdoor Fun and Safety

Playing outside on a sunny day can be a delightful experience both for the children and for you. Rolling a ball back and forth with a toddler and playing catch with older children in the yard or in a nearby park are nice ways to spend an afternoon. Other popular outdoor activities for kids include hopscotch, jump rope, and kickball. Ask the parents if their children are allowed to roller-skate or ride bicycles up and down the block.

Entertaining a child outdoors does not have to be complicated. Taking walks around the neighborhood can be an adventure for him or her. See how many blue cars you can count on one street. Point out all the different kinds of flowers growing on nearby lawns or in gardens. Time how long it takes to walk—or skip or jog—once around the block. Stopping at a pizza parlor or an ice cream shop on the way home is a fun treat, and sometimes parents are willing to leave extra money for such outings. And don't forget the playground! There's nothing like a super slide and some swings to brighten a kid's day.

Outdoor activities come with their own set of dangers, however. Make sure not to play near traffic and

Playing outside on a nice day can be fun, but if you are walking or playing in the street, you should be hyper-vigilant for vehicles.

not to let the kids wander too far. Always remember to hold the child's hand when crossing the street and never to cross against the light. If a car comes speeding toward you out of nowhere, a child might not be able to run as fast as you to avoid it.

Sometimes children want to invite their friends over to play. Check with the parents first, and then decide if you are willing to accept the added responsibility of caring for another child. If you are the only adult in the house and have agreed to the play date, you need to understand that you are now responsible for the safety of both children.

Whatever you decide to do with a child is time well spent if he or she remains happy and safe. Children will cherish these moments for a long time and won't dread the days when their parents have to leave them for a little while. You may also find that you gain personal satisfaction from knowing that you have brightened a child's day.

Chapter 4

Keeping Your Cool with the Kids

Natasha is baby-sitting for the first time. She has some experience watching her younger brother, but she has never baby-sat for anybody else. Ten minutes after Mr. and Mrs. Franklin leave the house, two-year-old Jack wakes up and starts to cry. The Franklins told Natasha that Jack had just been put to bed and would probably sleep through the night, but things have not gone as expected, and the baby needs his diaper changed.

Natasha picks up the baby and carries him over to the changing table. She has never changed a diaper before, and Jack will not stop crying. When Natasha finally does get the diaper on the baby, she realizes that it is on backward.

Baby-sitters should try to remain calm and in control when children act out or throw temper tantrums.

Just then, four-year-old Sarah, who had been playing quietly, starts screaming and throwing her toy blocks across the room. Natasha begins to feel as though she is losing control of the situation. She realizes that she needs to stay calm, so she takes a deep breath and finishes changing Jack's diaper—this time getting it on right. She picks the baby up from the changing table, and walks over to Sarah.

Natasha knows that Sarah just wants attention. In a soft yet firm voice, she explains to Sarah that it is not nice to throw things. She tells Sarah that she had to change her brother's diaper and that until she gets Jack to fall asleep again, Sarah will have to play by herself. Natasha sets out some toys for Sarah to keep her busy for a little while.

Within a few minutes the baby falls back to sleep in Natasha's arms, and Sarah settles down with a teddy bear and a puzzle.

Baby-sitters take on a lot of responsibility when they agree to watch someone else's children, and they have to be prepared for unexpected complications. Natasha was looking forward to a nice, calm evening, with one child already asleep and the other playing quietly by herself. It is easy to panic when circumstances suddenly change and you are surrounded by crying children who don't know you very well. Even experienced sitters sometimes feel overwhelmed by unexpected events. Remember, though, that your reaction will have a major effect on how the children react. No matter how frightened you feel inside, always appear calm and confident so that the children feel safe. If you show that you are panicking, the children will panic too.

It is important to stay cool in all situations. Never raise your voice in front of a child who is scared or injured. If you feel that you are losing control of a situation, make sure that the children are in a secure place (either a crib or a playpen) and that they are not hurt, and then close your eyes and count to ten. If you feel that you have to leave the room, walk into the hallway or another room for a minute and take a deep breath. This will give you a chance to refocus and stay relaxed.

Dealing with Bad Behavior

Sometimes children misbehave because their parents are not around and they want to test a new baby-sitter's limits. They want to see how far they can push you before you get angry. A child may yell at you or refuse to listen to your instructions. He or she may even try to hit you. The first thing to remember is that it is never acceptable to hit a child for any reason, no matter what he or she has done. You are in charge, but you are not the parent; you don't get to make that kind of decision. Something else to keep in mind is that

As a baby-sitter, it is important to explain to the children that you care about their feelings and you want them to be happy.

you should never shake a child. Children's bodies are much more fragile than adults'. Their skulls are still developing, and shaking a child can cause permanent brain damage.

This does not mean that a child should be allowed to hit you or get away with inappropriate behavior, however. The best thing to do when a child is throwing a tantrum is to give him or her a "time-out." This means that you instruct the child to sit in a quiet place—such as a chair, a couch, or even the kitchen table—for a set amount of time, usually around five minutes. Explain to the child that you understand that he or she is upset, but that his or her behavior is not appropriate.

After the child has had time to calm down, explain that you are willing to talk about whatever is bothering him or her. If you as the baby-sitter get angry, that won't solve anything. You need to let children know that you care about their feelings and that you want them to be happy, but that they can't act in any way they please just because their parents are not around.

Of course, this approach works only for children old enough to understand what you mean. A child over three years old should understand the purpose of a time-out, but a toddler may not. To discipline toddlers, explain to them that what they are doing is not nice. Toddlers often have temper tantrums. If this should happen and the child seems inconsolable, leave him or her alone for a while. Walk to another part of the room or even into another room in the house. When the child calms down, ask if he or she would like to play a game or read a book. There is no need to discuss the fact that the child just had a tantrum.

It is important to understand that children are never bad; it is their behavior that is bad. If a child continuously misbehaves, in certain cases it is permissible to take away some privileges. It is best to check with the parents beforehand, however. Remember, parents have certain ideas about how they want their children raised, and as their employee, you should respect their rules and decisions.

If a child doesn't want to finish his or her homework, you can explain that there will be no television until all homework is completed. You should never threaten to withhold meals as punishment, but if a child refuses to eat dinner, you can warn him or her that you will take away dessert if the behavior continues.

When a Child Fights with Another Child

Sometimes children fight with one another. They may have arguments with siblings or friends. In these situations, it is important not to take sides or show favoritism. Children are very sensitive, and their feelings can easily be hurt. Never embarrass a child. You want to make children feel good about themselves. Putting them down or insulting them will only make them feel worse and they may act out even more. If a child is hitting or causing harm to another child, it is important to separate them immediately. You can listen to both sides of the story and then try to come up with a fair compromise. If they seem to be fighting for no real reason, separate them in different rooms or try to redirect their attention by engaging them in fun and interesting activities.

As the person in charge, you need to establish your authority from the beginning so that the children will respect and listen to you. Children need to know what

One way to discipline a child is to explain that there will be no television until all homework is completed.

to expect, so try to be consistent and to keep your rules the same as the parents'. This includes rules regarding bedtime, television privileges, play dates, and any toys and games they are allowed to play with.

If you tell a child that you will take away a privilege if he or she misbehaves, it is important to follow through. If you just threaten, he or she will soon realize that you are not serious. If you say that a child can't have any ice cream until his or her toys are put away, stick to that decision no matter how much the child complains.

Nobody likes to take orders, and it's no fun being told what to do all the time. Instead, suggest alternatives. For example, you can say to a child, "If you don't want to share your crayons with your brother, you can play with your dollhouse." This way you are still in control, and no one feels slighted. Remember, everyone has bad moods once in a while, even children.

If a child consistently or seriously misbehaves while you are watching him or her, it is important to let the parents know. You don't have to mention every little incident, especially minor ones, but parents can discipline their kids much better than you can. You want to make sure that the child understands that you care about him or her, but that you mean business and that he or she has to listen to you or there will be consequences.

Chapter 5

Negotiating and Networking

So now you finally have your first baby-sitting job. The parents think you're great, and the kids adore you, but you still haven't talked about one important thing: money. Money can be a very uncomfortable topic to discuss, so it is usually best to let the parents bring up the subject first. Have patience. They want to make sure that you are the right baby-sitter for them. They will probably base your salary on your level of experience. And of course, they want to pay you the least amount possible for the best care.

Chloe walks into the Hasen family's home. The children greet her with hugs and immediately want to play. She knows the family from the neighborhood, but this is her first time baby-sitting for them. She is a little bit nervous, even though she knows that she can do the job well. Until now, Chloe has never discussed with the Hasens how much she is going to be paid. She doesn't even know what the going rate is for baby-sitting. She wants to say something to Mr. and Mrs. Hasen before they leave for the evening, but she does not want to seem pushy. Soon they are out the door, and Chloe has no idea what she is going to get paid for the evening's work.

Getting Paid What You Deserve

It is best to discuss the issue of money before you actually start baby-sitting. The parents might suggest a trial run in which you stay alone with the children for a short time to see how things work out. After this initial introduction to the children, if the parents have still not asked what you would like to be paid, then it is appropriate for you to bring up the topic.

It is always a good idea to come prepared, so do some research first. If this is your first baby-sitting job, you can't realistically expect to get paid top dollar. Find out the going rate for baby-sitters in your community. You can go about this in many ways: You can ask friends who already baby-sit what they get paid;

you can ask your parents what they think is a fair price to charge your clients; or you can ask neighbors who have children what they pay their baby-sitters. You can even ask your teachers or guidance counselors. Some of the organizations listed in the back of this book can also give you an idea of how much you should be earning.

Rates may vary depending on the time of day that you work. You may earn more money for watching the children during the day, especially if you are expected to pick them up from school or prepare meals for them. Nighttime rates may be lower if the kids are already asleep when you arrive. You may also decide that you want to charge according to the number of children you are sitting for. If a family has four kids, you may decide to charge them more than a family with only two kids. However, it is usually best to pick one rate and stick with it. That makes things easier for everybody.

As a new baby-sitter, it is important to remember that you are providing a service for these people. Most people are fair and understanding, but some may try to take advantage of the fact that you don't have much experience. If a parent offers you a rate that is not acceptable, politely tell him or her that you would really enjoy the opportunity to baby-sit for the family, but that you were hoping for a little more money. You may want to offer to start at the initial rate with the understanding that after a certain number of weeks, if things are going well, you will get a raise. This will show the parents that you are willing to compromise.

If you are a first-time baby-sitter and receive only one offer, you may want to accept the job—no matter what the salary is—in order to gain some experience. During this time you can look for other jobs that offer better pay. Remember, you are a businessperson now, and you have the right to a fair salary.

Payment Schedule

Payment schedule is another important issue that should be decided early on. If you are going to be working more than once a week, the easiest thing may be for you to get paid at the end of each week. If you decide to do this, buy a small journal to carry around with you so that you can keep track of your hours. If you baby-sit only on occasion, it is probably best to get paid at the end of each day.

Sometimes parents may say that they will pay you next time or that they don't have enough cash to pay you. They may ask if you would mind waiting. This can be an uncomfortable situation. If it happens once or twice, let it go and be sure to get your money next time. If this seems to happen often, let the parents know that you need to work out a payment schedule with them.

Posting signs in your community or networking with adults is a good way to find baby-sitting jobs.

Branching Out

Once you have gained some experience, how do you go about expanding your business? The first place to start is with the people for whom you already baby-sit. Ask them if they know anyone else who is looking for a sitter. Chances are, if they like your work, they will recommend you to others. Reassure them that you will still be available for them when they need you. Sometimes people don't like to share their baby-sitters because they are afraid that the sitter will receive better offers or won't be around when needed. Tell the parents you work for that you won't let this happen. Loyalty to your clients is a sound practice in any kind of business.

Finding baby-sitting jobs will become a lot easier once you have some experience. You can post signs at the local library or community center, or in your building or apartment complex. These signs should state the approximate times that you are available, any baby-sitting experience you have, and the time of day you can be reached along with a phone number. You can also ask the parents of children you know if they will post flyers in their child's school. Some schools have a special bulletin board for such listings. You can also contact baby-sitting agencies; some of them are listed at the end of this book. These organizations can help you find jobs in your community, and they often screen both the parents and the baby-sitters to make sure that both parties are reliable and trustworthy.

One of the best ways to find a baby-sitting job is by word of mouth. This means letting people know that you are interested and telling them to keep their eyes open in case something comes up. These people don't even have to have children of their own, as long as they know people who do. Of course, the best way to get recommended for other jobs is to be an amazing baby-sitter. If you prove to people that you enjoy what you do, you will soon be picking and choosing your own jobs. The best part is that you'll get to set your own rate.

Chapter 6

Careers in Child Care

Not only can baby-sitting earn you extra money, it can also provide you with experience necessary for careers later in life. There are a variety of well-paying professions out there for people who love to work with children.

Jessica has always loved children and knows she wants to have a career someday that involves being around and caring for them. "What else can I do beside baby-sitting though?" she asks herself. "I want to have a full-time career with kids, not just a part-time, after-school job."

By going to the library and doing research on careers in child care, Jessica learns that baby-sitting has turned out to be more rewarding than she thought. The experience she has gained gives her a perfect starting point for any number of careers working with children. She has the opportunity of being a child caregiver, which is like baby-sitting but more involved. She can be a children's librarian, which will give her the opportunity of sparking their interest in reading and learning. She can also be a pediatrician or a child psychologist, both of which will allow her to take part in children's health, which she loves as well.

From doing a little research, Jessica has learned that the baby-sitting job she started out doing for a little extra money has turned out to be a great springboard for a fulfilling career.

Child Caregiver

A child caregiver's job is similar to a baby-sitter's, except that a caregiver is more involved in the growth and development of the child.

Caregivers can work almost anywhere. Homes, schools, religious institutions, workplaces, shopping malls, and hospitals are a few examples. Caregivers who work in private homes are sometimes called nannies. Nannies care for children on a twenty-four-hour basis, attending to all of their needs, including bathing, feeding, clothing, and taking them to and from school.

If you really like working with children, you may decide to become a teacher, which will enable you to positively influence the lives of many children.

Part of the caregiver's job may also involve keeping records of the child's development. He or she may track the child's grades at school, medical records, or after-school activities such as sports. The caregiver may also be involved in helping the child get along with other children, develop good verbal skills, and practice good personal hygiene.

Both the child and the parents depend heavily on the caregiver. Expect to always be on call. This may become stressful, but being this involved in a child's life is also very rewarding. You will become closer to the family than you would as a baby-sitter. You will also be more involved in the child's personal development. If you love to watch children grow and mature, caregiving is an excellent profession to pursue.

Children's Librarian

It is very important that children become interested in reading at an early age. As a children's librarian you will help foster children's interest in books and learning by conducting reading groups, teaching them how the library is organized, and showing them where and how to find information. The interest in books and learning you create will stay with them throughout their lives, helping them excel both at school and in their future careers.

To learn more about how to become a children's librarian, see the Web site for the American Library Association, which is accessible through an Internet link provided in the back of this book.

Pediatrician

As a pediatrician, or children's doctor, you will be mostly involved in children's physical development and well-being.

Good physical health is developed from an early age. As a pediatrician you will teach children how to maintain a healthy lifestyle by explaining the value of nutrition, how to exercise, and how to stay fit throughout their lives.

Pediatricians generally have a more challenging job than doctors who treat adults, because children have a harder time explaining aches and pains. They may also not want to be at the doctor's office in the first place, making it hard for the pediatrician to do his or her job. People who become pediatricians, however, often like this challenge.

Child Psychologist

A child psychologist, on the other hand, deals only with the mental health of children. Catching psychological problems at an early age can prevent a number of problems down the road.

Some issues that a child psychologist might deal with are autism, attention deficit disorder (ADD), speech and language disabilities, learning disabilities, mental retardation, dyslexia, and behavioral disorders, to name a few.

Like a caregiver, a child psychologist has the opportunity to work in a number of places, including hospitals, schools, summer camps, day-care centers, and private practices. There are also a number of disorders in which a child psychologist can specialize such as cerebral palsy and Down's syndrome. A child psychologist may also work with particular types of children such as the gifted and talented.

There are many careers available for people who love children and want to be involved in their health and development. Baby-sitting is an excellent place to start. As a baby-sitter you will be introduced to a demanding but rewarding responsibility. Not only will it allow you to be a part of a child's development, but it will also help you develop as a person.

Glossary

acquaint To get to know someone or something.

antiseptic A type of medicine, usually applied to the skin, that prevents infection.

curfew A time, usually in the evening, when one must come home.

inconsolable Unable to be comforted or made to feel better.

negotiate To discuss an issue in order to reach an agreement.

privilege A special right or favor granted to someone.

reference A source that can offer information about the character and ability of a person.

resilient Having the ability to bounce back easily.

tantrum An outburst of rage.

trustworthy Reliable.

Where to Go for Help

To find first-aid and CPR classes in your area, contact local colleges or community centers. You can also look in the phone book under Safety, Education, or Instruction.

Baby-Sitting Training Courses

American Red Cross Babysitter's Training Course
(ages 11 to 15)
For more information, contact your local American Red Cross chapter or the agency headquarters:
American Red Cross
Attn: Public Inquiry Office
1621 North Kent Street, 11th Floor

Arlington, VA 22209
(703) 248-4222
Web site: http://www.redcross.org/services/hss/
courses/babyindex.html
The American Red Cross also publishes the
Babysitter's Handbook, which can be ordered
through your local Red Cross chapter.

Safe Sitter (ages 11 to 13)
To find the location of the Safe Sitter class nearest
you, write, call, or e-mail the headquarters at:
5670 Caito Drive, #172
Indianapolis, IN 46226
(317) 543-3840
e-mail: safesitter@netdirect.net
Web site: http://www.safesitter.org

Web Sites

Due to the changing nature of Internet links, the
Rosen Publishing Group, Inc., has developed an online
list of Web sites related to the subject of this book.
This site is updated regularly. Please use this link to
access the list:

http://www.rosenlinks.com/ntk/baby/

Video

The Teenager's Guide to Successful Babysitting by Tina Viereborne, in association with American Production Services and American Video Productions, 1997.

For Further Reading

Barkin, Carol, and Elizabeth James. *The New Complete Babysitter's Handbook*. New York: Clarion Books, 1995.

Beecham, Jahnna, and Malcolm Hillgartner. *Guide to Baby-Sitting* (The Baby-Sitters Club). New York: Scholastic, 1996.

Burgeson, Nancy. *Baby-Sitter's Guide*. Mahwah, NJ: Troll Associates, 1991.

Dayee, Frances S. *Babysitting*. New York: Franklin Watts, 1990.

Kuch, K. D. *The Babysitter's Handbook*. New York: Random House, 1997.

Litvin, Jay, and Lee Salk. *How to Be a Super Sitter*. Lincolnwood, IL: VGM Career Horizons, 1991.

Marsoli, Lisa Ann. *Things to Know About Babysitting.* Morristown, NJ: Silver Burdett, 1985.

National Geographic Society. *A World of Things to Do.* Washington, DC: National Geographic Society, 1987.

Zakarin, Debra Mostow. *The Ultimate Baby-Sitter's Handbook.* Los Angeles: Price Stern Sloan, 1997.

Index

About the Author
Aileen Weintraub is an editor and writer residing in Brooklyn, New York. She has authored *Everything You Need to Know About Eating Smart*, *Choosing a Career in Child Care*, and *Choosing a Career as a Nurse-Midwife*.

Photo Credits
Cover, pp. 2, 14, 19, 28, 36 by Thaddeus Harden; pp. 6, 10, 33, 39, 42, 48 by Maura B. McConnell; p. 30 © Corbis; p. 53 by Cindy Reiman.

Design
Thomas Forget

Layout
Hillary Arnold